No More Milk

Sundress Publications • Knoxville, TN

Editors: Sara Henning & Erin Elizabeth Smith
Editorial Assistant: Jane Huffman

Special Thanks to Graham Bonnington & Montreux Rotholtz.

Colophon: This book is set in YuMincho.

Cover Image: Gabrielle Montesanti

Cover Design: Kristen Camille Ton

Book Design: Erin Elizabeth Smith

No More Milk
Karen Craigo

Table of Contents

For Mike:
human kindness.

Down Will Come

I'm really not much
of a singer. Tonight
I rockabye the baby just
the way you'd rock
a truck from a snowdrift,
grinding gears over
lowest notes, rumbling
the infant to sleep.
I'll admit I get by
on the general notion
that any mom singing
is holy. Was there ever
such music as your own
mother's voice, filtered
through the drumhead
of her sternum, growl
of song and blood
and breath? And even
if it wasn't beautiful then,
it is now, in memory,
her real voice a bough
breaking crisp on the phone
hundreds of miles
from where you fall.

Milk

Last night, a baby cried
outside my window and I knew
I should be holding it.
I was sure she was talking
to me, my own baby,
a thousand miles away,
grown hazy, not clear
like that music from the courtyard.
I brought the hand pump
in my suitcase and it took all day
to draw an ounce.

My baby and I are near the end.
It's no one's fault. Each day
I have less to give.
When I heard that baby's
terrible song, I wanted
to go to her, give to her.
And I cried a little, the way
mothers cry, and catch it,
and place it in smallest mouths,
so this morning there was a glass of it,
of milk—what the body repels
as it pulls the other to us.

The world is dense with hunger.
Sometimes I have to pull
my baby's fist from his mouth
just to feed him,
and I am mindful that for some
hunger is a fist that never stops

being a fist. What I'm trying to say
is I couldn't dump that milk.
For the baby in the courtyard,
for my baby, for all
the babies, I drank it down.

Hours after Anger, He Wakes Me

My son wakes me to tell me
I terrify. *I feel like I'm sinking
into the world*, he says, hard
to understand through tears.
What could I do but apologize
to this sweetest part of myself,
rub his back with heavy strokes,
hold him here with me, and down.
He spilled his milk today, or rather
he left it where his brother
could crawl to it, pull it to him
with curious hands—this, after
several warnings, delivered, I think,
gently. I could have kissed him,
cleared away the milk, aware more
spills would follow. But he sobbed
through sharp instructions, cleaned
it up, and now I know between us
there will be no more milk.
It's true that I'm fearsome,
much as my own mother raged.
It worked for her, mostly—
a matter of style, of which
I have none, no go-to plan,
no particular talent for this,
truth be told. And I have strange
ideas about prayers—who it is
that listens, and whether or how
they work—but my son is now
sleeping, and I know this as grace,
so I offer one: vague, no words,

almost an odor of regret and shame.
I stayed awake to write this poem
and to draw a symbol on the fat
wedge of my thumb—a secret mark
that means *Love the boy better,*
keep him, pin him to this Earth.

Rockabye

Someone inside me is upside
down. Someone inside me waits.
Someone calls me his pillow. Someone
thinks he's a whale.
                        He hears me speak
through saltwater, begins to see color
through black. Someone
bicycles feet; someone
punches a bag.
                        Someone's
been singing a shanty. Someone
has rocked me to sleep.
Someone flexes his hands—fingers
tally the wall.
                        Someone is naked
but warm; someone tethered
composes a song. Someone's bough
can't bear his weight.
                        Someone
makes ready to fall.

Three Tips for Inhabiting Our Material World

A shelter made of dirt
is still a shelter—my son
tells me this, calls it
a pro-tip, one
among dozens he spins
out of air. Later,
he'll sit on the red chair
and say, *You may notice*
this is a fake red chair,
like a fake milk pitcher
that can also be used
for root beer—each tip
so like a sequin
I hold it in my fingers,
turn it to pan the light.
Some days he comes home
and the first thing he does
is pull from his pocket
a feather. He smuggles
these to me in secret,
like the code
to a lock, and I keep them
in a vase—glorious
tail feathers, pin feathers,
scraps from a wing.
He knows I love these
artifacts of flight or battle,
prismatic, pocket-bent
or frayed. Another tip:
An ice cream truck
is not an ice-cream truck—

15

I mean it is not a truck
made out of ice cream.
He is working on a notion
of place—about where
we might settle together,
and with what
we may line our nest.

How We Save

We bought the bank to teach him
thrift. Sometimes he gets a dollar
for doing a household thing—
he'll schlep items to their rooms,
thus saving me the effort.
And so I slip him a dollar and
he folds it, tucks it in the pig,
and it's there, his money, bent
but crisp, with a little change.
And once in its place, wings—
a note, folded twice, in the jar,
IOU and a sum, what it cost
to fill the car and take him
where he wanted to go.
So little is free but a few things
come close, like when we drove
to the park, walked to its hidden
meadow, and lay down together
in the grass the day he blessed
it with a name—*Place of Fresh
Butterfly Milk*—as if a butterfly
were a thing that could nourish.

Special Money

It's true I've broken down, paid
for a gallon of milk wholly
in Bicentennial quarters.
And I forget why I let go
of the Kennedy half-dollars
the tooth fairy once deposited
in my bank of pillows.
But there are bills to pay,
and they can be satisfied
with wheat pennies, or in
Susan B. Anthonys, or
the two-dollar bills my parents
brought me from the track.
Nothing is so special it can't
be made bread. Remember
when they changed the money,
how quickly the old bills
vanished, the modest faces
of presidents replaced
with robust twins?
Now you never see
those small-faced bills,
except a few I saved
and timidly presented in order
to restore the cable. I'm not sure
if my son remembers the folio
of quarters his grandma gave him,
fifty of them, one for each state.
I wonder if he'd miss Alaska.

Micromanaging the Garden

for Mike

The purple things stay. I like
how the stalks grow, crookedly tall,
wherever the heck they please.
You're not sold on them,
and you're the one determined
to work the dirt, to move things
from here to there, willing them
to thrive. I like the slugs
as much as the lilacs, and I admit
this works against me. I just
want something to grow here,
and it should be beautiful
in its dailiness, and durable,
surprising. We can examine
each green shoot and question
whether plant or weed, and either way,
do we desire them, because desire
can turn one to the other.
You keep saying you're going
to dig up the thistle from the lot
of that closed-down store,
then plant it by the fence out back.
I have my doubts, but it's not me
out there on my knees.

Naming What Is

for Aimee and Dustin

You picture them in the garden:
a nameless animal presses its face
against her hand, and she offers
a syllable or two. The man with her
agrees: *dog, monkey, snake.* It was all
so pure then—they were incorruptible,
and language moved between them
like a beast, sweet and lumbering.
You can see them: a man and a woman,
in a grove, all of the trees laden with fruit.
There is a pond there, and one bird, yet
to be christened, stretches to touch
a white neck. It takes two to make language,
and the animals were just the beginning.
Did they label how the nighthawk veers
through the dusk, or that splash the man hears
when it's too late to spot the lake trout
twisting in air? There is so much
waiting to be named—we are surrounded
by things anonymous and strange for their lack.
And even now two heads bend together
in whispered negotiation. Their very prayers
acknowledge the power in the name:
Berry. Woman. Swan. Man. Miracle.

Self-Portrait as Woman Driving 80 mph

Somewhere near Des Moines you work it out,
that truth that you have traced in highway lines:
with God and love there is no room for doubt.

For both you've labored and for both you've knelt
in stones, and both you know to be unkind,
but somewhere near Des Moines you work this out:

it's not the mere litany of "thou shalts"
that brought you to this leaving state of mind.
With God and love there is no room for doubt,

for wondering what the hell it's all about.
They're what you flee and what you need to find,
somewhere. Near Des Moines you work it out,

this calculus of faith that runs throughout
your life and has you running, fighting blind
with God. And love, there is no room for doubt

in your Volkswagen. No one hears you shout
a name to cows and thundering combines.
Somewhere around Des Moines you work it out:
with God and love there is no room for doubt.

Haiku, Late Summer (A Prayer)

Father, forgive me
for wavering unfaithful
here, amid sparrows.

Someone's radio
just won't quit playing love songs.
Leaves pin me to grass.

I've cut down an elm
to carve out a monument
to scattered petals.

Lightning in the west
advances this direction,
cracks in the ceiling.

Let me use plain words:
I don't think I can handle
this autumn alone.

The leaves curl upward,
have learned to count on each drop
of water you give.

At the Food Bank

A couple times I went there.
I was hungry and more: I wanted
something lovingly offered, grace
I didn't have to sweat for.
Those days my skin was enameled
in grease from standing at the fryer,
pulling up basket after basket
before the long walk home.
It wasn't a job that could be said
to help anyone, to do anything
good, although who doesn't like
fries when they're hot and salty,
not snuck, but served in the open
on the side of something more.
At the food bank they gave me
cans and pasta, day-old bread,
and, when I was lucky, roadkill—
a deer or an elk, something else
that had given up on foraging.

Scat with Mourning Dove

I wake to syncopated song,
a kiss, whisker sharp, a body
warm against mine. It is the bird
that has made us rise, trilling jazz
like Ella Fitzgerald, and we join
its refrain, yesterday's anger
reduced to syllables in the air.
How often we wake like this
and the first sounds we make
are air bursting from lips,
wind like a high hat
between tongue and roof of mouth,
the "bah" and "pah" and "doot"
we can't keep our mouths from forming.
Nonsense hangs with the sun
just over our pillows. It is not too early
or too late to make music.
The bird makes the melody
and we join her, marveling again
how God made us, made jazz,
made an instrument of a dove.

Before We Try "I Love You"

We've tested the word obliquely.
On the phone, buffered by a dozen states,
we've admitted we'd love to be together,
that we're lovers, that there are things
we love, each about the other. So easy,
affirming our fondness for football,
for chocolate, for the road that links us, for days
like today. But when we speak of each other,
something catches the word at the trap door
of our throats. It's like that egg
the magician deposits in the cave of his ear,
then draws whole from his mouth.
Seems impossible, something so large, hiding
in the space above the tongue. We suspect
a kind of trickery, until he cracks it into a glass
and we see it, a sun bobbing through its own
clear sky. We love days like that—
how everything seems possible and everything
surprises. Think of the finch, singing
by your window—how his burst of song
first amazes you, then strikes you as
the only thing he could possibly sing,
the only thing that makes any sense at all.

Guided Meditation: Inventory

1. Feet

Focus your attention
on the feet—street urchins
who cleave to you,
skinny, knobbed,
bearing their history
as a fear of stones.
You are lying
on your side, bones
of your feet stacked
like woodpiles.
All of your walking
confuses your feet,
who think you're trying
to leave them. Recall
the places your feet
have carried you:
down cobblestones,
across shallow rivers,
into and out of
all kinds of shit.
Touch the pure
curve of an instep;
rub your thumb
over calloused heel.
Apologize for shoes,
for your poor sense
of direction. True,
the world will give up
its carpet tacks,

its broken glass,
but promise the feet
you'll be vigilant.

2. Legs

Focus your attention
on the legs—spindles
that bear the heft
of you. Let the ankles,
graceful as the neck
of the Madonna,
flop outward in repose.
Relax your calves.
Note the bruises
on your shins. Think
of your efficient,
secretarial knees,
how they record
a sideways tally
each time you fall.
You think you've got
the legs all figured out.
Truth is, you hardly
know them.
How is it thighs
that have scissored
grown men, left them
gasping for air,
ever failed to carry
you from harm?
Resolve to forgive
your body. It's getting
too old for conspiracy—
some mornings it balks
at standing, at carrying you
to the kitchen for coffee.
Start here, then,

just below your cleft.
Think of happier times:
the radial kisses,
the dear hands pushing
at your knees.
Bear in mind
for the body, pink
pantsuit the spirit wears,
this is all there is.

3. Hips

Move your attention to the hips. They are broad.
They turn slowly like a beam from a lighthouse.
Imagine you can open them to the light. You can't.
Your pelvis is solid, the body's firm cradle.
But you can invite yourself to settle in, to curl up
like a cat in an inglenook. There is even a fire.
It burns red in you.
     Settle down. You don't have
to be empty. You can fill you. You can invite
others in. Any time you feel closed or hollow,
remember, there is a secret door, a room.

4. Hand

Now consider the hand,
its fingers, the nails of them,
even the hangnails you bother
with your teeth. These
are the body's workers.
They burrow in gardens
or butt-cracks, flick spiders,
untangle knots.
You have cursed them
for not being able
to open a jar, for not
learning how to knit.
Don't forget it's hand
against hand that offers
the body's first thrill.
Old workhorse body—
do you even remember
that once you walked
beside a boy, hand tingling
at your side, brushing
against him, willing him
to take it? This body
has come a long way
since then, but when
you focus you can still
feel his nervous steam

as he purled his fingers
into yours. Finally.

5. Arms

Think of the arms:
how they've carried
potatoes, folding-chairs,
your dying dog.
Bless them for trying
to hula, for the times
they flew a kite.
There was a first time
they straightened
to hold you up. Once
they pulled a woman
wide of harm;
once they threw a man
down some stairs.
It's all about leverage.
They've cradled
cut flowers and cradled
a bone. For you
they've tunneled
into holes and when
you cross them
they're a pile of sticks.
They've reached up
and come short.
They've airplaned.
They've loved the way
arms do, tight.
Not all they've done
is righteous,
but bless them.
Picture them moving
along the gantry

of your shoulders.
They're snapping
a bedsheet.
They're pulling
two corners
together.

6. Throat

Focus your attention
on the throat: storehouse
of the body's rage. Sometimes
it flies from you unbidden, at strangers
in cars, at God.

Only the mute can make a go
of love. Your throat scratches
and clears, truth skitters
like a mole rat, and all the things
you should have said
calcify, *I'm sorry* lodged
like a chicken bone.

Poor throat. Even now
I can hear it trying to sing.

7. Head

Consider the variable weight
of the head—days you couldn't lift it
from your pillow, others it thrilled
like a parade balloon. Ignore
the mug. Note only that your eyes
turn green when they cry. A mechanic
in the brain drops a scrim.
Yours has never been a head
for dancing. You specialize
in cobwebs and trying to dislodge
true words—chiseled plates litter its floor;
you wanted *margarine* but said *Magellan*
and were left to circumnavigate dry toast.
You can hear a rattle when you nod.
You bow beneath the burden of words.

8. Crown

There is a part of you
that isn't—just above
your scalp, violet halo, region
of angels and mad cartoons,
always just about to blow.

Focus your attention there.
Lift yourself to it. I think
hope lives there, or love—
things that have no place
near the body's rags and bruises,
its churlishness and fear.

Crow's-nest for the pirate ship
you maraud in, pointed, always,
toward higher ground.

In Praise of the Body Broken in Two

I woke this way—bent
at the waist, vibrating,
a silver chime struck
with a hammer.
For three days, I cradled
my body in my arms,
carried it swaddled
from room to room, pain
tolling like a temple bell.
How could I not love any warm thing
breathing against my chest—
how not love what's helpless,
a wounded animal you feed
with a spoon?
Usually the body prefers
to drag itself from room to room
and declines my offer
of help. Pain, in the end,
is personal. Sometimes, though,
I'll lean against my shoulder,
and side by side I'll make my way
from bed to toilet to couch.
It is no longer in me
to wish to leave the body, be spirit
soaring above self.
The body is not a wrapper
to be discarded.
Count me among those
locked out and gazing
at the architecture of skin
and bones—the arches and rose

windows, buttresses, crockets, cusps.
This place is so holy
you'd have to leave your shoes
to step inside.

Death by Bleeding

You've thought of it, but no:
the wrist is a narrow, helpless thing,
and you have traced its rivers
through the skin. All morning
you've been flexing your hand,
and you've seen in those cords
a dear throat, clearing. How
would you survive the streets
of heaven if your hands dangled
helpless at your sides? This
is how God debases us:
He finds us starving in wilderness
and tosses our bread to the dirt.
And if we try to hide
some of what's left it turns
to a bag of worms. In Jerusalem
there are trees so old
they have known the brush
of His hem. You picture
a redwood, but no—these
are stunted, twisted things,
curving in on themselves,
a terrified wringing. It's no stretch
to see yourself on your knees
in heaven's back alley,
snuffling for manna
like a dog. Should you see Him,
you'd have no defense, except
for the one the trees knew.

Death by Bullet

Alive, we can only conceive
of the searing. But there's a kind
of genius the doomed know—an idea
planted deep and guarded.
It blooms there, sudden metal flower.
I heard of one who survived:
the bullet glanced a molar, ricocheted,
left a mouse hole in his cheek.
Imagine the man's astonishment
as he stood there dead
and breathing. For too long
we've believed death is a host
who has to take us in, a guide
who won't leave us in the woods.
And then there's Sarai, too old
for nonsense—she laughed
at God's pronouncement.
When the seed took sudden root
in her, it must have felt this way—
hot revelation, sudden light
that changes you forever.

Death by Water

You imagine the ark
from the outside, the way
most people saw it—shuttered,
huge, already starting to stink.
And there you are beside it,
treading water, reaching
to touch the hull, your throat
raw from pleading.
Most of us lead dry lives,
which is why this is the death
we were born to. Inside
we're water and bones,
and so we bob on the waves
like a bag of sticks. Once,
all humanity was a forest, felled.
You can put your head under
and remember: didn't you surge
into this world on a wave, crying,
with your mouth full of salt?

Death by Fire

At the base of the flame
there's a blue answer.
If you look without blinking
you'll know its pattern,
remember the skin
of the man you love,
how it once glowed gold
against the sheets.

When Joseph's brothers
proclaimed him dead,
they brought their father proof:
his gaudy coat in shreds.
Jacob, unraveled, each day chose
a different thread to grieve to.
Near the end his torment
blazed red.

There's something
that stays behind us when we go,
if only for a time. Tell me how
to bloom like that. Should
I touch a candle to my skirt?
Or will there be a door
of flame to run through?

Walking the Labyrinth

Today I sat in a pew
and looked hard at the back
of your head—the part
that thins, that's hard to reach
with a comb, and where hair
swirls in a loop from its source.
I've made the mistake
of staring at your eyes.
Pardon me for saying it,
but the eyes are difficult
to love. You pin me there,
convex, hands forward
like a supplicant's.
The Earth is easy. It moves
along a twisted groove
and when I step into the woods
it is quiet, then noisy
with birdsong. All around
trees creak and I think I hear
them grow. But someone
has cut you uneven.
Your head is tipped
to listen and I follow
your cowlick's path.
I'm beginning to think

I could love you like this,
that it would be a start.

Gathering Eggs

I open a door, no bigger
than this notebook, and out
they rush, in a panic for dirt.

I'm here for their eggs,
a thing they give easily,
and I get it: some months
entire paychecks are taken
by snake-fingered hands.

There is the matter of food
and water. I scan the pen
for the sly fuck-you of yard-eggs.

I wonder if they saw
the meteor last night, fast-
skidding like a stepped-on yolk,
but these are early birds, bent
on the business of scratch.

In their boxes I measure
the heat of their orbs.
One girl waits me out—
quiet-sings her egg song,
eyes me as I back away.

Shell Money

In some places currency
began as mollusks. That sounds
like the work of a poet,
spying a shell, lifting it high
to declare this glistening thing
a thing of great worth. Once,
its value was known only
to the snail. Evicted,
she must have felt keenly
its merit. Woolf knew.
All you need is a room,
a little something to keep you
fed, but the shell is both chamber
and allowance. We poets excel
at declaring the worth
of small things. The value
of the cowrie starts and ends
in the pleasure of its finder,
or in the mollusk that perfectly
fits within its walls.

What It Means to Wait

You count out coins for a jug
of milk—that's what it is
when you work for tips.
Your purse weighs down
your shoulder, and you always
have something, no matter
the day of the week. Go deep,
you might find what you need.

Seems like everyone likes
that joke—palm your dollar
from the table and slip it
in a pocket, just a way to pull
your chain. They never forget
to put it back, and they grin,
no harm, but their prints
are all over your money.

In Search of the Right

On the way to Provincetown
I train my eyes starboard
willing to the surface
the fluke. The bay is a smooth
road. Nothing breaks its surface.
The sky, blue-gray, at times
merges with it. Not far
from here, the Stellwagen Bank
feeds the few right whales
that remain, and tourists
ride out to them in charters,
try to goad the holy with a stick.

We all want to be regarded
by a great lashed eye, and I
have erred so magnificently
that only in the largest lens
may I hope to find a speck of favor.

I'd like to believe
in blessings that find us
slantwise—that peer at us
obliquely, so sometimes
we don't even know
we're being regarded.
It's possible that far beneath

the surface, they cross
my path like cats.

The World You Recognize

One afternoon,
driving, you
look up and see
the moon, nearly full,
so frail against the sky
as to be almost
transparent.
Even more impossible:
that for a moment
you could fix your eyes
on the way the road,
polite, skirts an elm,
and when again
you see that
pale fraction, you
can't find it.
You've lost the moon—
a thing so large
it has its own gravity.
Maybe it's forgivable
to be disoriented
by woodsmoke
rising from
the pile of brush
a farmer has pulled
from his windbreak,
or by the circling dives
of the kestrel.
It seems everything
has become miniaturized—
the kestrel the smallest

of hawks, the ancient
forest reduced to a line
of useful trees.
The moon, too,
appeared reduced.
The shadows
of its dry seas exactly matched
that background where
it hung so precariously.
It is a fact
of afternoon driving
that sometimes you come
to a blind curve
and see clearly
the falling away of
the world. You recognize
that feeling—how
you could lie
in the back seat,
certain you were
standing still,
watch how the planet
blurred past
your window.

To the Goldfinch Outside East Hall

Say someone finds you
helpless—listing

on the sidewalk,
and above you a bank

of windows, flat
and gleaming like sky.

She will carry you in:
you will be dazed,

and by some reflex
you will hold her

with the narrow roots
of your toes. The fact

that you are golden
is of consequence:

it is difficult to hide
in low places, though the top

of the ash seems heavy
with your kind. On the ground

you were a comma—
brilliant pause in the gray.

It is sudden: your eyes
go round, you hunch down

and then fly beyond reach.
When you find yourself

in those windowless rooms, what
wouldn't you knock against

to return to her,
that pale version of you

who waits, trembling,
in a tree? In the end

you'll find the window
and you'll swim out to her

in the usual undulating way:
some wingbeats, small plunge,

and again, again, again.

Love Poem to the Symbols of Our Incompetence

The hand can cut like a knife,
but look at you, standing there stunned,
flinging guts of tomatoes
from your fingers. I've seen you
fuck up dinner, perplexed
by your still-uncooked potatoes,
checking your watch as if
they've missed an appointment.
Who continues to let you near the oven,
sad maroon, dumping noodles
all over your floor? I'd like to suggest
we order in tonight. As yet
there is no gadget to replace you
behind the wheel—you with the depth-
perception and muscle control
of an infant. Why are you working
so hard? Is there no one who loves you
sufficiently, no one who sees the danger
you face as you reel from room to room?

Walleye

I'm trying very hard
to be that true—
to try on the river
like a gray cloak.
I've seen how it carries
sticks down its length,
and faith says it does so
even as I sleep
by its side. I see
a message here:
that water is all
that remains to hold me,
hold me up.
If all I'm afraid of
is pain, there's nothing
to be afraid of:
how many times
have I loaded my pockets
for simple love
of stones—their edges,
the way they fit
in my palm?
Today the walleye spawn
so close to my front door.
I think I'm starting
to feel it—what it is

that pulls them so far
from their easy lake.

Ars Poetica

I want to say this
simply: I was out
near the river; the trees
were bare, and would be.
I saw no blacksnake
in the undergrowth,
but that doesn't mean
it wasn't there, all mouth
and narrow appetite,
nosing the dirt.
I could feel all
I was losing: I was
a hollow tree, enough space
beneath my sternum
for a nest. There was no one
to hold me but the world,
the empty air. Couldn't
it be love that makes
the cardinal stand,
a fresh wound
against the sky?
Could love make you
sing like that—
desperate, terrible?

What I Love about My Body

I love how it sits roundly,
a warm stone, when it is calm,
its waters stilled. How
it is pleasant to touch, free
of sticks and arrow points.
Humble, it stays until summoned,
but would happily serve,
glad pillow for you to rest on.
I love how it continues
to trust each new chair,
though it has been deceived,
perplexed in the splinters.
I love its terrible pants.

One Hundred Grand

for the $31.25 I have on me

I haven't told you, but I carry dollars,
folded crisp, in this pouch I wear.
The thinking is that the law
of attraction will kick in, and soon
I'll be swarmed with greenbacks,
ungainly as a mantis in flight.

Ever fork over a five-spot, thinking
you'd grabbed a one? That must be
what happened to the Woodrow,
a hundred thousand captured
in one bill, because there was a time,
I guess, when it needed
to be portable. You'd walk down
the boulevard, buying mansions,
tossing scraps of green
in your very own ticker-tape parade.

Wilson looks dubious,
the adjusted value of that rectangle
close to two million today. He peers
through an almost-invisible pince-nez,
barely comprehends. Me,
I'd like to have a bill like that,
just touch it, green on the obverse,
orange in back, like a rare moth
too gorgeous for the pin.

Late Afternoon, Shadows

You are not as tall
as you appear, nor nearly
so thin; it's just how the sun
has cast its shadows.
Your father is dying.
That's a fact, hard and chill
as the places wind has shaved the snow
into a crust you could walk on.
Be thankful winter has found you—
it has given you a reason
to avoid indifferent light,
to stay in bed, declining calls,
to ignore teakettle hysteria.
What could have made you step
into the coldest light
the day had to offer?
Look at what you've made
of your fear, stretching
across an acre of gray. See
how the corn stubble
has pierced you?

Half-Buried

Eyes-down is how you see
the nests of things, the slim tail
slipping to undergrowth.
Out of everyone who walks
this trail, I'm likeliest to spot
the tresses of the abandoned,
the betrayed body decaying
under ferns. Yes, the sky
has something to offer—
clouds and crows and hedge-
apples—but underfoot, things
take cover and breathe
where our boots pass, beside
the tiniest of blossoms.
Sometimes I'll see a heart
embedded in the path,
but when I pull it from dirt
I lose it—it's just a rock
balanced in my palm,
maybe more a symbol
of the beloved for its weight
and its solidity.
My pocket is fat with tokens.
At home, I have bowls of them—
stones shaped like stones
where once someone saw
a flash of something more.

Offering

Good measure, pressed down,
shaken together, running over,
will be put in your lap.
　　　—Luke 6:38

Last week I put stamps
in the offering—a useful
sort of gift, the kind
I'd want a God
to value.

I've given less,
given more, like
a gift card for ice cream,
or all the change from
the bottom of my bag,
two fistfuls, and if God
blessed me, surely
some treasurer
did not.

One Sunday
I wrote a poem
and set it there
on the stone faces
of currency.
I suppose someone
had to tally the value
of that.

Taproot

Sometimes the phone rings
twice an hour, and we don't
pick up, no more to give
at two-thirty than two,
and three o'clock looks
very much the same.

The trees teach little about debt
but draw themselves upward.
If something blocks their light
they'll grow around it.

Deep in the ground,
the roots go straight down,
or spread, or pull up knees.
They point themselves
directly at their need.

We'd like to find
an answer in the world,
but honeysuckle shrugs,
and the stare of the io moth
gives nothing away.

Time Is Money

I'm not sure what time it is,
an hour misplaced between
phone and laptop, and it's never
been my habit to keep a watch.
So here I am in the middle
of time, both early and late,

but with nothing awaiting me,
so it might be said I have all
the time in the world. Strange
way we have of putting it.
I would never hoard time.
Someone might need it, like I

once did, to study the starfish
hand of a brand new boy, or
to count backwards as
the hockey game concludes,
the rocket ship ignites. How
will they launch the silver cup

if I won't relinquish time?
And anyway, I'm not convinced
it's what we think it is—
some thread we roll up
in a skein until we reach
the frazzled end of it.

Time is more like that time
I dropped cornstarch in
the Amish store. The stuff

went everywhere, no matter
more resistant to gathering
in a pile, and soon other hands

were helping, pushing the grains
into a mound, those hands
attached to cuffs of dresses
held together with straight pins,
anachronistic, pushing away
time and invention because

zippers and buttons are proud.
And look how my attention
has wandered from our pile of time,
and the stubborn particles of it
that don't make it to the mound
but escape into woodgrain

and refuse to be pushed.
A figure in black wields
a dustpan, and there goes
our metaphor, or most of it—
into a bin, not cosmic,
but corrugated and clean,

behind an Amish counter,
and those who saw it work
on forgetting the particulars,
keep only a keener understanding
of supernovas. All I'm wanting
is to know what time it is,

which device to put faith in.
I have work to do, a storehouse

to fill, and time is something
finer and faster than sand,
and I've seen, oh, I've seen
how it gets away from us.

Your Love as That Poster of the Kitten in the Tree

for RJ and Michael

What drew you there
is obvious. There was the sky,
and morning light in the sky,
all mellow and golden,
and there were flowers,
dogwood, strangely, flinging
their scent to the wind.
And there was a toehold, a way
to raise yourself higher,
and another and yet another,
a path to a clearer point of view.
Think of that air, blossoms
all around, and how always
there is a branch leading
higher. It is well
worth the climb, worth
holding on with all
you or anyone
has got.

Poem on My Coffee Break

Today I'm fitting in a poem
on the back of an envelope,
something folded in my purse,
pencil breaking on the flap.

It's meant for official business,
and I'd owe someone $300
if I mentioned how I love the way
the sun through the trees
spots my son, little leopard,
off to school. The IRS requests
consideration for the road
he walks there, for the school,
for fighter jets and space toilets.

It's a mixed bag, isn't it,
what we get, and even what
I carry in this purse, not
quite as empty as it feels.

Look—I found a mint.

Evanesce

Used to be our worth was easy
to measure—a coin for each eye,
or one placed above the tongue.
Those were the chips we had
when we rose from the table
and wandered off in search
of something better to do.
I guess this is what remains
when the earth pulls us in,
but isn't our value in the loam—
how we make the ground
a little softer with our going?
Then someone walking past
can look down and say wait,
here's some neat old money.

Fruits

I want to say something
about the wild strawberries—
how they were all along the path
and seemed new. The field guide
says April and May, but this
is the red heart of June, and there
they were, so bright, unusually small.
We weren't sure what we were seeing—
even after I kneeled to touch one
and noted the surface studded
with seeds. You could walk by them
at a clip and not see.
Once you do, they're stoplights,
blinking in the undergrowth.
But this baby won't quit crying—
I think a tooth is trying to bloom
in his inconsolable mouth
like the white blossoms we missed,
the ones that announced the berries.
They're what I think about
in my second hour of rocking
as the baby flexes his back
and lifts his mouth closer
to my ear. The baby says beauty
is ephemeral, and the earth
rewards us when we pause
before its fruits. Go ahead and write,
he says—tell the people
what you know. It's entirely possible
those berries are already gone.

Acknowledgements

Atticus Review: "Milk," "To the Goldfinch Outside East Hall,"
    and "Death by Bleeding"
Blue Lyra Review: "Naming What Is"
Cave Region Review: "In Search of the Right"
Contemporary Verse 2: "What Change Is" and "Shell Money"
Crab Orchard Review: "Scat with Mourning Dove"
Friends Journal: "Evanesce"
Gargoyle: "Time Is Money"
Hobart: "Ars Poetica" and "Fruits"
I-70 Review: "Hours after Anger, He Wakes Me"
Kettle Blue Review: "Half-Buried"
The Lake: "Down Will Come"
Mantis: "The World You Recognize"
The Merton Seasonal: "Self-Portrait as Woman Driving 80 mph"
Pirene's Fountain: "Three Tips for Inhabiting Our Material World"
Prairie Schooner: "Death by Bullet," "Death by Fire," and "Death
    by Water"
Redactions: "Micromanaging the Garden"
Spoon River Poetry Review: "In Praise of the Body Broken in Two"
Suburban Diaspora: "Taproot"
TAB: A Journal of Poetry & Poetics: "Before We Try 'I Love You'"
    and "Haiku, Late Summer (A Prayer)"
Truck: "Gathering Eggs"

The poems "Walking the Labyrinth," "Meditation," "Naming What Is,"
"Death by Bleeding," "Death by Fire," "Death by Bullet," and "Death
by Water" appeared in the Winged City Chapbook Press chapbook
Someone Could Build Something Here. "Death by Water" was also
reprinted in *As It Ought to Be*. "Milk" was reprinted in *New Poetry
from the Midwest*. Parts of "Guided Meditation: Inventory" appeared in
the anthology *Parts of the Whole* as "Meditation." "Your Love as That
Poster of a Kitten in a Tree" was reprinted in *Escape Into Life*.

About the Author

Karen Craigo is the author of two previous chapbooks, *Someone Could Build Something Here* (Winged City Chapbooks, 2013) and *Stone for an Eye* (Kent State/Wick, 2004), and her work has appeared in numerous journals. She is a freelance writer and editor and a writing instructor in Springfield, Missouri, and she maintains *Better View of the Moon*, a daily blog on writing, creativity, and publishing matters.

Other Sundress Titles

Theater of Parts
M. Mack
$15

Suites for the Modern Dancer
Jill Khoury
$15

Every Love Story is an Apocalypse Story
Donna Vorreyer
$14

What Will Keep Us Alive
Kristin LaTour
$14

Ha Ha Ha Thump
Amorak Huey
$14

Stationed Near the Gateway
Margaret Bashaar
$14

major characters in minor films
Kristy Bowen
$14

Confluence
Sandra Marchetti
$14

Hallelujah for the Ghosties
Melanie Jordan
$14

Fortress
Kristina Marie Darling
$14

When I Wake It Will Be Forever
Virginia Smith Rice
$14

The Lost Animals
David Cazden
$14

A House of Many Windows
Donna Vorreyer
$14

The Hardship Post
Jehanne Dubrow
$14

The Old Cities
Marcel Brouwers
$14

One Perfect Bird
Letitia Trent
$14

Like a Fish
Daniel Crocker
$14

The Bone Folders
T.A. Noonan
$14

CPSIA information can be obtained
at www.ICGtesting.com
Printed in the USA
BVOW08s1039271116

469011BV00001B/49/P

9 781939 675392